The Night Before

Two Christmas Eve Services With Children's Sermons

Rod Tkach
Jeffrey A. Whitman
Wesley T. Runk

CSS Publishing Company, Inc., Lima, Ohio

THE NIGHT BEFORE

For more information about CSS Publishing Company resources, visit our website at www.csspub.com or e-mail us at custserv@csspub.com or call (800) 241-4056.

Cover design by Barbara Spencer
ISBN 0-7880-2381-0   PRINTED IN U.S.A.

Table Of Contents

A
Christmas
Gift

A Complete Service
For Christmas Eve

Rod Tkach

*To my mom who introduced me
to the world of words,
and to my bride who believed
in the dream of appealing
to the heart through word
and imagination
for the sake of the kingdom.*

Contents

A Christmas Gift
Order Of Worship

Gathering Music

Call To Worship
Leader: Come, peek into the birthing room of the Savior.
People: A hospital it is not: no beepers, no buzzers, no doctors or nurses.
Leader: Listen. You can hear the sounds of Bethlehem, a tired country community.
People: The contractions are becoming more frequent. It's time.
Leader: Joseph, without the benefit of Lamaze, beholds a miracle.
People: Tired and relieved, Mary tenderly nurses Immanuel.
Leader: The Savior is born! Come and worship.
People: We come to worship Christ, the newborn King.

Christmas Carol   "Angels From The Realms Of Glory" (vv. 1, 2, 4)

The First Present

Scripture Reading   Luke 1:26-38

Meditation   "The First Christmas After"

Lighting Of The Advent Candle   Candle Of Faith
     The Advent wreath reminds us that the living God takes the initiative and is willing to enter into relationship with us. Faith, that expression of trust or belief, comes out of a context of awe. That is, an awareness of our being called upon. The faith candle is the light of God who comes calling upon our hearts with their hurts and darkness. The first candle reminds us that the birth of the Savior was an act of God's faithfulness.

Christmas Prayer
     In the midst of the pain, Lord, it is difficult to hear the angels sing. Yet, the words of the Christmas carol remind us of God and sinners being reconciled. Give us the faith to embrace your offer of peace. Help us to be sensitive to those who struggle with this first Christmas after. May you come as the Prince of Peace we so desperately need. Amen.

Christmas Carol   "Hark! The Herald Angels Sing" (vv. 1, 3)

The Second Present

Scripture Reading   Luke 1:39-45

Meditation   "A Christmas Question"

Lighting Of The Advent Candle   Candle Of Hope

The greenery of the Advent wreath speaks of the new life brought by the God who comes. The evergreen is an expression of hope. Hope is a desire whose fulfillment is cherished, an expectation of receiving something good from God. The candle of hope gives expression to that deepest of desires: eternal life. A hope that finds fulfillment as the hopes and fears of all the years are met through the hope of glory, Jesus the Christ.

Christmas Prayer

Precious Lord, forgive us where our actions and words deny the hope that people desire. For we, too, long for a reason to hope. And then, in all our hopelessness, you come to us through the Holy Child of Bethlehem. Give us the grace not only to receive this gift of hope but to share it with others as well, through Christ our Lord. Amen.

Christmas Carol   "O Little Town Of Bethlehem" (vv. 1, 4)

The Third Present

Scripture Reading   Luke 2:1-7

Meditation   "A Christmas Bag"

Lighting Of The Advent Candle   Candle Of Love

The Hebrew verb for love means to breathe after or to delight in. The third candle reminds us that God takes the initiative in seeking us because he longs for a relationship with us. His steadfast love — with its expressions of compassion, charity, power, and tenderness — endures forever. From the very beginning, God has been in search of us. His love could have it no other way. The third candle reminds us that his love came down at Christmas.

Christmas Prayer

Love came down at Christmas, O God, so we may come home. Help us let go of the things that we bag up and that prevent us from coming home: the anger, the bitterness, the grudges, or the desire for revenge. Enable us to have a bag filled with forgiving love as we take the Christmas story home with us, in the name of Christ we pray. Amen.

Christmas Carol   "Love Came Down At Christmas"

The Fourth Present

Scripture Reading   Luke 2:8-12

Meditation   "A Christmas Quest"

Lighting Of The Advent Candle   Candle Of Joy

Joy is scripturally defined as delight, gladness, or exuberance. Through hope with its healing and peace with its forgiveness, the joy of Christ becomes real to us through the love of God. This joy is not dependent upon circumstances. Rather, it is dependent upon the person of Jesus Christ who is always with us as God's gift. The candle of joy reminds us of this gift who brings joy to the world.

Christmas Prayer

Almighty God, how often we are disappointed when Christmas fails to live up to expectations. Forgive us, for we are quick to see what it isn't instead of seeing the miracle that is: the coming of the Christ! Help us to be captivated by the joy of Immanuel, of having God with us! For it is in his name that we pray. Amen.

Christmas Carol   "Joy To The World" (vv. 1, 4)

The Fifth Present

Scripture Reading   Luke 2:13-20

Meditation   "A Christmas Fiction"

Lighting Of The Advent Candle   The Christ Candle

The true light of Christmas is not found in the fictions of commercials and culture. Rather, it is found in Christ the King, whom shepherds guard and angels sing. The light of the Christ candle illuminates the candles of faith, hope, love, and joy. For each of the other candles finds its fulfillment in the one who comes as the Light of the World: Jesus the Christ.

Christmas Prayer

What child is this who can make God real to our hearts? Who can take us beyond the fictions of Christmas and usher us into the very presence of God? Lord, we long for the reality of Christmas. It's so easy to get caught up in the busyness of it all that we miss you! Forgive us, we ask, and renew the true meaning of Christmas in our hearts. Amen.

Christmas Carol   "What Child Is This"

Presenting Our Present

Receiving Of Christmas Offering

God so loved the world that he gave his only Son. The offering this evening continues that mission of sharing Jesus with our world. Let us pray:

From deep within the recesses of your heart, O Lord, your love came to us that first Christmas. The joy of Immanuel, of God with us, is for all the world. So move in our hearts that through this offering many may hear the good news of Jesus, our Savior. Amen.

(The ushers come forward to receive the offering at this time.)

Offertory   "The First Noel"

Giving The Present Of The Light Of Christmas

Lighting Of Individual Candles

Jesus, born in Bethlehem, is the light of the world. So it is that our light comes from the light of Christ. As we share the good news of Jesus the light spreads. The light from the Christ candle will be shared from the pastor to the ushers and then to the congregation as we sing verses one and four of "Silent Night."

(The ushers come forward to light their candles.)

Christmas Carol   "Silent Night" (vv. 1, 4)

(Stand in silence as organ plays another verse.)

Benediction

May the faith that sees us through the first Christmas after, the hope that lives in the Christmas question, the love symbolized in a Christmas bag, and the joy discovered through a Christmas quest be yours as you go in the truth of Christmas; that of Immanuel, God with us. Amen.

Recessional Music

Meditation 1
The First Christmas After

The "First Christmas After" gives expression to that strange mixture of emotion that comes with the first Christmas after losing a loved one. In the midst of the anticipation and joy of the season, it's easy to lose sight of those having a blue Christmas. This contemporary psalm of lament may just help us to be mindful of those with hurting hearts.

The first Christmas, O God of my father, came out of the blue,
Each of us in our private world wondering what to do.
The traditional pageantry of the Christmas story began to unfold
In spite of Mary and Joseph's faith, we found little to hold.

The first Christmas the children's program went off on cue
But the absence of his presence was felt by those who knew.
How could they sing with such joy and such grace
When the songs reminded us of his embrace?

The first Christmas was just going through the motions
Ambivalent to all the commotion.
The family gathered for the traditional meal,
Which made his absence even more real.

O God, is your advent under the tree?
Do you have any idea how much this family needs thee?
You've not been present in candle, sermon, or song
Everything about this Christmas seems so wrong!

Is there anything that can deliver us from this despair?
Where is that majestic song in the air?
With angelic good news on a starry night
Of a Savior who can make things right?

O God, break your silence on this night
Let some sense of joy be a revealing light.
For more is at stake than presents under a tree
It's a question of whether faith will meet life eternally.

The first Christmas, after the stories began to be told,
Unwrapping memories more precious than gold.
Before we knew it, there was laughter from the heart
The God of Christmas was giving us a new start.

A Christmas Question

Christmas Eve was only a day away. Cars were backed up for blocks, to the point that even the interstate exit ramp was a waiting line. Not only did you need the patience of Job to reach the mall, it took even more to find a parking place. There it was! Just as we started turning, a car whose plates read "H O P E" cut us off. The kids gasped as Christmas cheer became a backseat jeer. The wise man behind the wheel said, "I'm tempted to give them a piece of my mind. Instead, I'll practice what their license plate says and answer their bumper sticker about Jesus." So, Dad honked the horn!

The game plan was simple: divide and conquer. Each parent would take one of the younger kids while the teens did their thing. In an hour they would reconnect at the food court. "Toys R Gone" would have been a more truthful advertisment. Hopes and dreams became hopeless nightmares as the quest for the year's hottest toy seemed futile. Carts crashed and tempers flared, especially in the NASCAR section. It was then that the five-year-old asked, *"Is this Christmas?"*

Tired and worn, part of the family camped out at a table while the others worked their way toward refreshments. Cold Cokes in Christmas décor and hot pretzels with icing sounded so good. The teen girls working the counter were frazzled. The order for the customers in front of us was wrong and their change was incorrect. After the order was straightened out, the customers did the strangest thing. With a smile, they gave the waitress a big tip! Hope leaped into her eyes. Looking up at Mom, the six-year-old asked, *"Is this Christmas?"*

What a great question! The time out allowed us to reflect. One of the teens asked, "Do you suppose this is what it was like at tax time in Bethlehem?" The other replied, "If finding an inn is like finding a parking space, no wonder there was no room!" As the conversation continued, we became absorbed in noticing how the Christmas story intersected with our own story. We talked, we laughed, and with hope renewed we set out to finish the list.

Only this time it was with a dual purpose: to finish shopping but to also intentionally share the gift of hope through random acts of kindness. Giving hope to others helped us to answer the question: *"Is this Christmas?"*

Meditation 3
A Christmas Bag

It happened every Christmas growing up. The trauma of Christmas program practices was followed by the sheer panic of the program itself. Would the children remember their parts? Would they speak loud enough to be heard? Would those few boys blessed with extra energy be still long enough to be shepherds? Or would they run down the aisle yelling at a pretend wolf to bring back their sheep? No one said anything, though many wondered what their father, the pastor, thought.

It happened every Christmas growing up. The kid's anxiety concerning the Christmas program was nothing compared to the adult leaders. An unspoken worry filled the air as the unanswered questions were about to be answered. Would that cute, shy little girl be able to say her part this year? Or would she pull her dress over her head to hide like last year? Being the daughter of the superintendent of Sunday school didn't help either!

Then it happened, right on cue. The sanctuary lights were dimmed. The front of the church was transformed as props and characters almost magically appeared. Suddenly, lights flooded the front of the church. Make no mistake about it. It was show time! There was laughter, applause, and a wave of recognition as little ones spotted Dad and Mom or Grandpa and Grandma in the audience. The time flew by and before you knew it, the program was over.

And that's when the Christmas bags appeared. The dreams of Legos and Barbies were momentarily put on hold. Each child was given a brown Christmas bag filled with peanuts, an apple, an orange, a red and white candy cane, and sometimes a popcorn ball. The men of the church handed them out like they contained great treasure. The love that went into the bags was often met with looks of bewilderment. What did these bags have to do with Christmas?

The love shared at Christmas has to do with giving. The Christmas bags came from a simpler time. There wasn't the money to do Christmas the way it is so often done today. Yet, the joy of giving was experienced through the sacrifice that made the bags possible. The joy came in seeing the smiles of the children who first received the bag, and so it became a tradition. But if the tradition is to keep its meaning, then the story must be told. The story of love changed that bag from a bag of peanuts to a Christmas bag of love. Are you sharing the story of love behind your traditions of giving?

Meditation 4

A Christmas Quest

With great excitement and anticipation, the family headed into the hills in search of the *perfect* Christmas tree. The amused adults were content to watch as the cousins ran in the snow from one possibility to the next. A freshly fallen snow blanketed the barren trees as they shivered in the frigid December wind. The pines basked in the warmth of their snow-white stocking caps and the capes of green.

The tree had to be the best Christmas tree ever. The ones the boys found were awesome. Perfect in every way, if Rockefeller Plaza or the Washington Mall were the destination. If only there were a way to squeeze one of these gorgeous giants into the cozy home where Christmas was to be celebrated. The girls claimed to have found the most beautiful tree in the forest and it was the right size, too! It wasn't open to debate, either. The wood saw coming out of the trunk verified that the dads agreed.

Pulling into the driveway should have signaled the end of a great adventure, but triumph turned to tragedy as the snow was shaken out. The most beautiful tree turned out to be the ugliest, scrawniest Christmas tree one could imagine. It made Charlie Brown's Christmas tree look good! Not even decorations could hide all the open, barren spots. How could there be Christmas joy when the tree brought tears to the eyes just by looking at it?

Then it happened: wire, the drill, a trimmer and the branches trimmed so that the tree would fit into the stand all magically appeared. Could the tears of disappointment be turned into smiles of joy? Could disappointment be turned into delight? Or sadness into gladness? Could one of the dads really build a live Christmas tree? Within an hour holes were drilled, branches were trimmed and wired into place. The eyes of hope and hands of faith were bringing joy to life as the tree changed before our very eyes.

It's easy to overlook the little things, or to settle for the way things are. But sometimes the joy of Christmas is found in the little things that can be changed for the better. There have been a lot of Christmas trees in the decades since the quest, but that tree is etched into the memory because of the quest and the joy of the tree's transformation. Joy that's at the very heart of Christmas.

Meditation 5
A Christmas Fiction

Behind the Music is a popular television show that takes the viewer past the glitz and the glamour. The narrator reveals the true story that lies behind the perceptions and fictions. Behind the fictions of Christmas are some amazing truths, but we have to get beyond the power of fictions' grip if we are to experience the mystery and miracle of Christmas.

One Christmas fiction is that Christmas has always been celebrated the way it is now. Stepping behind Christmas, we see that for the first 300 years of Christianity, Easter was the major focus. It wasn't until the conversion of Emperor Constantine that Christmas began to take center stage. A mid-winter festival was already being celebrated in the empire. Rather than dismantle it, Constantine co-opted it with the festival becoming a celebration of Jesus' birth! That's the origin of the December celebration.

Stepping behind the fiction of Christmas we discover that the baby Jesus actually cried in spite of what the Christmas carol says. How else could he let Mary know that he was hungry or Joseph know that it was time for a diaper change? Or take the three kings; the Gospel of Matthew says they were Wise Men or Magi, not kings. We assume that because they presented gifts of gold, frankincense, and myrrh that there were only three. But there could have been more, as scripture doesn't say. Besides, they found the child and Mary in a *house*! So they didn't exactly show up on Jesus' birthday.

In the classic "'Twas The Night Before Christmas," Saint Nick is described as a little old driver, so lively and quick. So how did Saint Nick morph into Santa Claus dressed in Coca-Cola red and white? Ask the advertising department at Coke. It was a stroke of marketing genius. But, stepping behind the popular tradition we do discover there was a person named Saint Nicholas who had a gift for secretly giving gifts. The stories about him took on a life of their own with Saint Nicholas becoming larger than life. In the United States, Saint Nick became known as Santa Claus. Once again we discover our picture of Christmas being drawn from the music: Santa making a list and checking it twice.

One Christmas song declares that Christmas is for children. Yet, when we step behind the music we discover that the elderly played a significant role in the Christmas story. From Zechariah and Elizabeth opening their hearts and home to Mary, to Simeon in the temple who held the promised Christ, to the 84-year-old prophetess, Anna, who gave thanks to God. Anna spoke of Jesus to all those who were looking for the redemption of Jerusalem.

Christmas fictions. Yes, some of the traditions as currently observed are more fiction than fact. Yet, when we step behind the fictions there are elements of truth. Constantine's conversion initiated Christmas as we know it. What could be more appropriate than sharing the coming of the Christ into our own hearts as we gather for Christmas? When was the last time matters of faith were shared in the family or with friends?

Or take the statement *first we sing, then we believe.* What do the Christmas carols teach us about Christmas? Do a little research on a favorite Christmas carol. You may be surprised to discover that "O Little Town Of Bethlehem" was written by Philips Brooks as a gift for his Sunday school children. Take a look at the theology in "Hark! The Herald Angels Sing" as Charles Wesley describes the purpose for Christ's coming.

Or take the evolution of a Saint named Nicholas whose anonymous giving of gifts became known as Santa Claus. The point of Christmas fictions is not to point out the fictions. Rather, it's to put us in touch with the truths behind the fictions. When we take away the fictions of Christmas we are left with one undeniable fact: the birth of Immanuel — of God with us. The fictions of Christmas emerged to help celebrate that reality, not replace it. May that be true for us as well.

O Come, Emmanuel

A Candlelight Service
For Christmas Eve

Jeffrey A. Whitman

Dedicated to
Randy, Kelli, and Kendra

Contents

Introduction

"Our journey to Bethlehem begins with longing." These words set the tone for "O Come, Emmanuel," a moving candlelight service for Christmas Eve that uses the ancient Antiphons of Advent to explore the longing behind our search for the Messiah. As the service unfolds, the singing and the reading of each antiphon leads us to reflect on the hopes and desires that bring us to Bethlehem in search of the Messiah. When the announcement is made that God has come among us we respond with joyful song. The service concludes with a ceremony of candlelight and a call for all the faithful to come to God who in Jesus has come among us.

This service is designed for two readers and a quartet with opportunities for choirs to participate. The members of the quartet each sing one of the verses of "O Come, O Come Emmanuel" which is based on the Antiphons of Advent. Having the members of the quartet sing from different locations in the sanctuary adds dramatic effect to the service. I would suggest that the two women, the two men, and the quartet sing the verse together from the front of the sanctuary. The members of the quartet should sing without accompaniment and should not sing the refrain until the end of the service. I have included an arrangement of the "Christmas Antiphon" for the quartet to sing at the conclusion of the service following the Christmas Eve prayer. This antiphon serves as a response to the prayer and as an introduction to the closing hymn. I have also included a suggested organ introduction that leads the congregation from the end of the antiphon to the beginning of the hymn "O Come, All Ye Faithful." I would like to add my deep thanks to Kent Conrad for his assistance in the arrangement of this antiphon.

Two acolytes are used in this service and instructions for their participation are found in the script. No candles are lit when the service begins. The acolytes are asked to light candles throughout the service during the singing of the carols and anthems to symbolize the coming Jesus, the light of the world.

During The Ceremony Of Candlelight, for the sake of safety, remind the congregation to hold their lighted candles upright, and dip each unlighted candle into the flame of a lighted candle.

Other music choices will be left to the individual churches. One piece our church found very fitting was, "How Far Is It To Bethlehem?" arranged by Mack Wilberg.

O Come, Emmanuel
Order Of Worship

Christmas Eve Music

Gathering

Reading

Soloist Response

Reading

Carol   "Once In Royal David's City" (Alexander/Gauntlett)

(Solo)
Once in royal David's city
Stood a lowly cattle shed,
Where a mother laid her baby
In a manger for his bed;
Mary was that mother mild,
Jesus Christ her little child.

(All)
He came down to earth from heaven,
Who is God and Lord of all,
And his shelter was a stable,
And his cradle was a stall.
With the poor, the scorned, the lowly,
Lived on earth our Savior holy.

(Women)
And, through all his wondrous childhood,
He would honor and obey,
Love and watch the lowly maiden
In whose gentle arms he lay:
Christian children all must be mild,
Obedient, good as he.

(Men)
For he is our childhood's pattern,
day by day, like us, he grew;
he was little, weak, and helpless,
tears and smiles, like us he knew.
and he feeleth for our sadness,
and he shareth in our gladness.

(All)	And our eyes at last shall see him,
	Through his own redeeming love;
	For that Child so dear and gentle
	Is our Lord in heaven above;
	And he leads his children on
	To the place where he is gone.
(All)	Not in that poor lowly stable,
	With the oxen standing by,
	We shall see him; but in heaven,
	Set at God's right hand on high;
	Where like stars his children crowned,
	All in white shall wait around.

Responsive Prayer

Leader 1: Let us pray. O God of mercy and grace we lift our voices to heaven and await your coming. We long for heaven to touch earth. As we watch and pray we wonder with the psalmist: How long, O Lord, will you forget us? How long will you hide your face from us?

People: **How long must we bear pain in our souls, and have sorrow in our hearts all day long?**

Leader 2: Consider and answer me, O Lord my God! Give light to my eyes.

People: **For we have trusted in your steadfast love; our hearts shall rejoice in your salvation. We will sing to you because you, O God of salvation, will come and deal bountifully with us.**

Leader 1: O Come, Emmanuel. Amen.

O Come, O Wisdom

Reading

Soloist Response

Scripture   Isaiah 2:1-5

Bell Choir Anthem

Lighting Of Candles

O Come, O Lord Of Might

Reading

Soloist Response

Scripture   Micah 5:2-5a

Carol   "O Little Town Of Bethlehem" (Brooks/Redner)
O little town of Bethlehem, how still we see thee lie!
Above thy deep and dreamless sleep
the silent stars go by;
Yet in thy dark streets shineth the everlasting light;
The hopes and fears of all the years are met in thee tonight.

How silently, how silently, the wondrous gift is given!
So God imparts to human hearts the blessings of his heav'n.
No ear may hear his coming, but in this world of sin,
Where meek souls will receive him, still the dear Christ enters in.

O Holy Child of Bethlehem! Descend to us, we pray;
Cast out our sin and enter in; be born in us today.
We hear the Christmas angels the great glad tidings tell;
O come to us, abide with us, our Lord Emmanuel!

Lighting Of Candles

O Come, O Shoot Of Jesse

Reading

Soloist Response

Scripture   Isaiah 11:1-9

Solo   "How Far Is It To Bethlehem?" (English Carol)

Lighting Of Candles

O Come, O Key Of David

Reading

Soloist Response

Scripture   Isaiah 40:1-11

Carol   "It Came Upon The Midnight Clear" (Sears/Willis)
It came upon the midnight clear, that glorious song of old,
From angels bending near the earth, to touch their harps of gold:
"Peace on the earth, good will to men, from heaven's all-gracious king."
The world in solemn stillness lay, to hear the angels sing.

Still through the cloven skies they come with peaceful wings unfurled,
And still their heavenly music floats o'er all the weary world;
Above its sad and lowly plains, they bend on hovering wing,
And ever o'er its Babel sounds the blessed angels sing.

For lo! the days are hastening on, by prophet seen of old,
When with the ever-circling years shall come the time foretold
When peace shall over all the earth its ancient splendors fling,
And the whole world send back the song which now the angels sing.

Lighting Of Candles

O Come, Desire Of Nations

Reading

Soloist Response

Scripture   Isaiah 9:2-7

Anthem

Lighting Of Candles

O Come, O Dayspring

Reading

Soloist Response

Scripture   Luke 2:1-20

Carols To Celebrate The Coming Of The Messiah
Carol   "Angels We Have Heard On High" (French Carol Melody)
                    Angels we have heard on high
                    Sweetly singing o'er the plains,
                    And the mountains in reply
                    Echo back their joyous strains.
                    Gloria in excelsis Deo
                    Gloria in excelsis Deo

Shepherds why this jubilee?
Why your joyous strains prolong?
Say what may the tidings be,
Which inspire your heavenly song?
Gloria in excelsis Deo
Gloria in excelsis Deo

Come to Bethlehem and see
Him whose birth the angels sing:
Come adore, on bended knee,
Christ, the Lord, the newborn King.
Gloria in excelsis Deo
Gloria in excelsis Deo

Carol   "Good Christian Friends Rejoice" (German 14th Century)

Good Christian friends rejoice,
With heart and soul and voice;
Now give heed to what we say,
Jesus Christ is born today
Ox and ass before him bow
And he is in the manger now
Christ is born today, Christ is born today.

Good Christian friends rejoice,
With heart and soul and voice;
Now you know of endless bliss,
Jesus Christ was born for this!
God has opened heaven's door
And we are blessed forever more.
Christ is born for this, Christ is born for this.

Carol   "Hark! The Herald Angels Sing" (Wesley/Mendelssohn)

Hark! The herald angels sing,
"Glory to the newborn King;
Peace on earth, and mercy mild,
God and sinners reconciled!"
Joyful, all ye nations rise, Join the triumph of the skies;
With the angelic host proclaim,
"Christ is born in Bethlehem!"
Hark! The herald angels sing,
"Glory to the newborn King!"

Christ, by highest heaven adored;
Christ, the everlasting Lord!
Late in time behold him come,
Offspring of the Virgin's womb.
Veiled in flesh the God-head see;
Hail the incarnate Deity,
Pleased as man with men to dwell, Jesus, our Emmanuel.
Hark! The herald angels sing,
"Glory to the newborn King!"

Hail the heaven-born Prince of peace!
Hail the Son of righteousness!
Light and life to all he brings,
Risen with healing in his wings,
Mild he lays his glory by,
Born that man no more may die,
Born to raise the sons of earth,
Born to give them second birth.
Hark! The herald angels sing,
"Glory to the newborn King!"

Lighting Of Candles

Offering

Offertory

Offertory Response   "O Little Town Of Bethlehem"
For Christ is born of Mary, And gathered all above,
While mortals sleep, the angels keep
Their watch of wondering love.
O morning stars, together Proclaim the holy birth!
And praises sing to God the King,
And peace to men on earth.

Prayer

The Service Of Candlelight

Scripture   John 1:1-14

The Ceremony Of Candlelight

Carol   "Silent Night" (Mohr/Gruber)

Silent night, holy night, all is calm, all is bright
Round yon virgin mother and child,
Holy infant so tender and mild
Sleep in heavenly peace, sleep in heavenly peace.

Silent night, holy night, Shepherds quake at the sight,
Glories stream from heaven afar,
Heavenly hosts sing alleluia;
Christ the Savior is born! Christ the Savior is born!

Silent night, holy night, Son of God, love's pure light
Radiant beams from thy holy face,
With the dawn of redeeming grace,
Jesus, Lord, at thy birth, Jesus, Lord, at thy birth.

A Christmas Eve Prayer

(Extinguish candles)

Depart To Greet The Messiah

Solos

Carol   "O Come, All Ye Faithful" (Wade)

O come, all ye faithful, joyful and triumphant,
O come ye, O come ye to Bethlehem;
Come and behold him, born the King of angels;
O come, let us adore him, O come, let us adore him,
O come, let us adore him, Christ the Lord!

God of God, Light of Light,
Lo he abhors not the Virgins womb
Very God, begotten not created;
O come, let us adore him, O come, let us adore him,
O come, let us adore him, Christ the Lord!

Sing choirs of angels, sing in exultation,
Sing all ye citizens of heaven above!
Glory to God, all glory in the highest
O come, let us adore him, O come, let us adore him,
O come, let us adore him, Christ the Lord!

Child for us sinners poor and in a manger,
We would embrace thee, with love and awe;
Who would not love thee, loving us so dearly?
O come, let us adore him, O come, let us adore him,
O come, let us adore him, Christ the Lord!

Amen, Lord we greet Thee, born this happy morning,
Jesus to Thee be all glory given
Word of the Father now in flesh appearing;
O come, let us adore him, O come, let us adore him,
O come, let us adore him, Christ the Lord!

Postlude

O Come, Emmanuel
Script

Christmas Eve Music

Gathering

Reading

Leader 1: Our journey to Bethlehem begins with longing. It is a longing that began thousands of years ago with God's people struggling to live faithfully in a small country surrounded by larger and more powerful nations. Throughout most of their history they lived as a conquered people; their country occupied by a world power. When they were in exile they longed for their homeland. When they were occupied they longed for justice, security, and peace, but most of all they looked and waited for God to come and redeem them.

Soloist Response *(Bass — singing from the balcony)*

O come, O come, Emmanuel,
And ransom captive Israel,
That mourns in lonely exile here,
Until the Son of God appear.

Reading

Leader 2: Our journey to Bethlehem begins with a longing born in the feeling that life is incomplete and the peace, security, and contentment we seek cannot be purchased, or discovered, or earned, or guaranteed by any human agency — it can only be given by our God. We come tonight and join the multitude of the faithful who lift their eyes to heaven and watch and wait and pray for the coming of the Messiah.

Carol "Once In Royal David's City"

Responsive Prayer

Leader 1: Let us pray. O God of mercy and grace we lift our voices to heaven and await your coming. We long for heaven to touch earth. As we watch and pray we wonder with the psalmist; how long, O Lord, will you forget us? How long will you hide your face from us?

People: **How long must we bear pain in our souls, and have sorrow in our hearts all day long?**

Leader 2: Consider and answer me, O Lord my God! Give light to my eyes.

People: **For we have trusted in your steadfast love; our hearts shall rejoice in your salvation. We will sing to you because you, O God of salvation, will come and deal bountifully with us.**

Leader 1: O come, Emmanuel. Amen.

O Come, O Wisdom

Reading

Leader 2: As people living in an age of information we journey to Bethlehem seeking wisdom. We long to understand our world and our place in it. And so we lift our minds to heaven and pray, "O Wisdom, who came from the mouth of the Most High, reaching from end to end and ordering all things mightily and sweetly: Come, and teach us the way of prudence. Amen."

Soloist Response   *(Alto — singing from back of sanctuary)*

O come, O Wisdom from on high
And order all things, far and nigh.
To us the path of knowledge show,
And help us in her ways to go.

Scripture   Isaiah 2:1-5

Leader 1: The words of the Prophet Isaiah: The word that Isaiah son of Amoz saw concerning Judah and Jerusalem. In days to come the mountains of the Lord's house shall be established as the highest of the mountains, and shall be raised above the hills; all the nations shall stream to it. Many peoples shall come and say, "Come, let us go up to the mountain of the LORD, to the house of the God of Jacob; that he may teach us his ways and that we may walk in his paths." For out of Zion shall go forth instruction, and the word of the LORD from Jerusalem. He shall judge between the nations, and shall arbitrate for many peoples; they shall beat their swords into plowshares, and their spears into pruning hooks; nation shall not lift up sword against nation, neither shall they learn war any more. O house of Jacob, come, let us walk in the light of the LORD!

Bell Choir Anthem

Lighting Of Candles
(While the bell choir is playing, the acolytes light the single altar candles.)

O Come, O Lord Of Might

Reading

Leader 1: As people living in an age of violence we journey to Bethlehem seeking security. We long to live without fear, in a community of reconciliation with our neighbors, and so we lift our spirit to heaven and pray, "O Adonai and ruler of the house of Israel, who appeared to Moses in the flame of the burning bush and gave him the Law on Sinai: Come, and redeem us. Amen."

Soloist Response   *(Tenor — singing from middle of sanctuary)*

> O come, O come, thou Lord of Might
> Who to thy tribes on Sinai's height
> In ancient times once gave the law
> In cloud and majesty, and awe.

Scripture   Micah 5:1-5a
Leader 2:   The words of the Prophet Micah: But you, O Bethlehem of Ephrathah, who are one of the little clans of Judah, from you shall come forth for me one who is to rule in Israel, whose origin is from of old, from ancient days. Therefore he shall give them up until the time when she who is in labor has brought forth; then the rest of his kindred shall return to the people of Israel. And he shall stand and feed his flock in the strength of the LORD, in the majesty of the name of the LORD his God. And they shall live secure, for now he shall be great to the ends of the earth; and he shall be the one of peace.

Carol   "O Little Town Of Bethlehem"

Lighting Of Candles
(While the carol is sung, the acolytes light the window candles and one purple candle on the advent wreath.)

O Come, O Shoot Of Jesse

Reading
Leader 2:   As people living in an age when the gap between the rich and poor continues to widen and an individual's worth is too often determined by the color of their skin, the language they speak, their gender or sexual orientation, we journey to Bethlehem seeking justice. We long to live in a world of shalom where all people are treated with love, respect, and dignity. And so we lift our eyes to heaven and pray, "O Shoot of Jesse who stands as a sign for all the people, before whom the kings keep silence and unto whom all the nations make supplication: Come, and deliver us without delay. Amen."

Soloist Response   *(Soprano — singing from front of sanctuary)*

> O come, O Shoot of Jesse free
> Thine own from Satan's tyranny;
> From depths of hell thy people save,
> And give them victory o'er the grave.

Scripture   Isaiah 11:1-9
Leader 1:   The words of the Prophet Isaiah: A shoot shall come out from the stump of Jesse, and a branch shall grow out of his roots. The spirit of the LORD shall rest on him, the spirit of wisdom and understanding, the spirit of counsel and might, the spirit of knowledge and the fear of the LORD. His delight shall be in the fear of the LORD. He shall

not judge by what his eyes see, or decide by what his ears hear; but with righteousness he shall judge the poor and decide with equity for the meek of the earth; he shall strike the earth with the rod of his mouth, and with the breath of his lips he shall kill the wicked. Righteousness shall be the belt around his waist, and faithfulness the belt around his loins. The wolf shall live with the lamb, the leopard shall lie down with the kid, the calf and the lion and the fatling together, and a little child shall lead them. The cow and the bear shall graze, their young shall lie down together; and the lion shall eat straw like the ox. The nursing child shall play over the hole of the asp, and the weaned child shall put its hand on the adder's den. They will not hurt or destroy on all my holy mountain; for the earth will be full of the knowledge of the LORD as the waters cover the sea.

Solo   "How Far Is It To Bethlehem?"

Lighting Of Candles
(While the soloist is singing, the acolytes light the candelabra on the altar and a second purple candle on the Advent wreath.)

O Come, O Key Of David

Reading
Leader 1:   As people too well acquainted with death we journey to Bethlehem seeking comfort in our grief. We long for resurrection hope in the midst of our despair as we remember the lives of those no longer with us, and so we lift our hearts to heaven and pray, "O Key of David, and Scepter of the House of Israel, who opens and no one can shut, who shuts and no one can open: Come, and bring forth those who sit in darkness and in the shadow of death. Amen."

Soloist Response   *(Tenor and Bass — singing from left side of choir loft)*
O come, O Key of David come
And open wide our heavenly home.
Make safe the path to endless day,
To hell's destruction close the way.

Scripture   Isaiah 40:1-11
Leader 2:   The words of the Prophet Isaiah: Comfort, O comfort my people, says your God. Speak tenderly to Jerusalem, and cry to her that she has served her term, that her penalty is paid, that she has received from the Lord's hand her sins.

A voice cries out: "In the wilderness prepare the way of the LORD, make straight in the desert a highway for our God. Every valley shall be lifted up, and every mountain and hill be made low; the uneven ground shall become level, and the rough places a plain. Then the glory of the LORD shall be revealed, and all people shall see it together, for the mouth of the LORD has spoken." A voice says, "Cry out!" And I said, "What shall I cry?" All people are grass, their constancy is like the flower of the field.

34

The grass withers, the flower fades, when the breath of the LORD blows upon it; surely the people are grass. The grass withers, the flower fades; but the word of our God will stand forever.

Get you up to a high mountain, O Zion, herald of good tidings; lift up your voice with strength, O Jerusalem, herald of good tidings, lift it up, do not fear; say to the cities of Judah, "Here is your God!" See, the Lord GOD comes with might, and his arm rules for him; his reward is with him, and his recompense before him. He will feed his flock like a shepherd; he will gather the lambs in his arms, and carry them in his bosom, and gently lead the mother sheep.

Carol   "It Came Upon The Midnight Clear"

Lighting Of Candles
(While the carol is sung, the acolytes light the pew candelabra and the third purple candle on the Advent wreath.)

O Come, Desire Of Nations

Reading
Leader 2:   As people living in an age of conflict we journey to Bethlehem seeking peace. We long to live in peace with our neighbors, our friends, our family, and other nations in the world we all share. And so we lift our spirit to heaven and pray, "O Lord of all the nations and the desired of all, the cornerstone who binds two into one: Come, and deliver us. Amen."

Soloist Response   *(Soprano and Alto — singing from the right side of choir loft)*
          O come, Desire of Nations bind
          All people in one heart and mind;
          Make envy, strife, and discord cease,
          Fill the whole world with heaven's peace.

Scripture   Isaiah 9:2-7
Leader 1:   The word of the Prophet Isaiah: The people who walked in darkness have seen a great light; those who lived in a land of deep darkness — on them light has shined. You have multiplied the nation, you have increased its joy; they rejoice before you as with joy at the harvest, as people exult when dividing plunder. For the yoke of their burden, and the bar across their shoulders, the rod of their oppressor, you have broken as on the day of Midian. For all the boots of the tramping warriors and all the garments rolled in blood shall be burned as fuel for the fire. For a child has been born for us, a son given to us; authority rests upon his shoulders; and he is named Wonderful Counselor, Mighty God, Everlasting Father, Prince of Peace. His authority shall grow continually, and there shall be endless peace for the throne of David and his kingdom. He

will establish and uphold it with justice and with righteousness from this time onward and forevermore. The zeal of the LORD of hosts will do this.

Anthem

Lighting Of Candles
(While the choir is singing, the acolytes light candles on the floor candelabra and the fourth purple candle on the Advent wreath.)

O Come, O Dayspring

Reading
Leader 1:   Our journey to Bethlehem begins with longing. We are drawn to the stable by our desire for wisdom, security, justice, hope, and peace which we cannot attain on our own. We come to Bethlehem longing for God to save us, and so we lift our souls to heaven and pray, "O Dawn of the East, brightness of light eternal, and Sun of Justice, Come, and lead us from our darkness to your eternal light. Amen."

Soloist Response   *(Quartet — singing from choir loft)*
    O come, O Dayspring, come and cheer
    Our spirits by Thine advent here.
    Disperse the gloomy clouds of night,
    And death's dark shadow put to flight.

Scripture   Luke 2:1-20
Leader 1:   Hear the good news: In those days a decree went out from Emperor Augustus that all the world should be registered. This was the first registration and was taken while Quirinius was governor of Syria. All went to their own towns to be registered. Joseph also went from the town of Nazareth in Galilee to Judea, to the city of David called Bethlehem, because he was descended from the house and family of David. He went to be registered with Mary, to whom he was engaged and who was expecting a child. While they were there, the time came for her to deliver her child. And she gave birth to her firstborn son and wrapped him in bands of cloth, and laid him in a manger, because there was no place for them in the inn.
Leader 2:   In that region there were shepherds living in the fields, keeping watch over their flock by night. Then an angel of the Lord stood before them, and the glory of the Lord shone around them, and they were terrified. But the angel said to them, "Do not be afraid; for see — I am bringing you good news of great joy for all the people: unto you is born this day in the city of David a Savior, who is Christ, the Lord. This will be a sign for you: you will find a child wrapped in bands of cloth and lying in a manger."
Leader 1:   And suddenly there was with the angel a multitude of the heavenly host, praising God and saying, "Glory to God in the highest heaven, and on earth peace among those whom he favors!"

Leader 2: When the angels had left them and gone into heaven, the shepherds said to one another, "Let us go now to Bethlehem and see this thing that has taken place, which the Lord has made known to us." So they went with haste and found Mary and Joseph, and the child lying in the manger.

Leader 1: When they saw this, they made known what had been told them about this child; and all who heard it were amazed at what the shepherds told them.

Leader 2: But Mary treasured all these words and pondered them in her heart. The shepherds returned, glorifying and praising God for all they had heard and seen, as it had been told them.

Carols To Celebrate The Coming Of The Messiah

"Angels We Have Heard On High" (French Carol Melody)
"Good Christian Friends Rejoice" (German 14th Century)
"Hark! The Herald Angels Sing" (Mendelssohn)

Lighting Of Candles
(While the carols are sung, the acolytes light the white Christ candle on the Advent wreath.)

Offering

Offertory

Offertory Response   "O Little Town Of Bethlehem"

For Christ is born of Mary,
And gathered all above,
While mortals sleep, the angels keep
Their watch of wondering love.
O morning stars, together
Proclaim the holy birth!
And praises sing to God the King,
And peace to men on earth.

Prayer

The Service Of Candlelight

Scripture   John 1:1-14

Leader 1: In the fullness of time, God came and dwelt among us. Hear the good news of the evangelist John: In the beginning was the Word, and the Word was with God, and the Word was God. He was in the beginning with God. All things came into being through him, and without him not one thing came into being. What has come into being in him was life, and the life was the light of all people. The light shines in the darkness, and the darkness did not overcome it.

Leader 2: There was a man sent from God, whose name was John. He came as a witness to testify to the light, so that all might believe through him. He himself was not the light, but he came to testify to the light. The true light, which enlightens everyone, was coming into the world. He was in the world, and the world came into being through him; yet the world did not know him.

Leader 1: He came to what was his own, and his own people did not accept him. But to all who received him, who believed in his name, he gave power to become children of God, who were born, not of blood or of the will of the flesh or of the will of man, but of God. And the Word became flesh and lived among us, and we have seen his glory, the glory as of a father's only son, full of grace and truth.

The Ceremony Of Candlelight

Carol   "Silent Night"

A Christmas Eve Prayer

Leader 1: O most gracious and merciful God on this holy night we journey with shepherds and Magi to the place where heaven touches earth and the Messiah is born. In holy silence we gaze in wonder at the mystery of your birth and the hope you bring to our broken lives. You have come bringing wisdom to enlighten our minds that we might understand our place in your world.

Leader 2: You have come to redeem us from our fear and free us to love one another as you have loved us.

Leader 1: You have come to establish your reign of justice for all people who you have created in your image.

Leader 2: You have come to be with those who are grieving that they might not be alone in their pain and to touch our brokenness with your healing hand.

Leader 1: You have come to bring us peace that we might learn the way of reconciliation and live together as your children in your world.

Leader 2: You have come O Holy One, to dwell among us, to save us from our self-destructive ways, to open our ears to hear your word of hope, to open our eyes to see signs of your presence in the brokenness of our world, to open our hearts that we may not live in despair but as those who have been redeemed. O come, O come among us now and fill us with your peace and joy. Amen.

(Extinguish candles)

Depart To Greet The Messiah

(See pages 40-43 for music for "Christmas Antiphon")

(Alto) O come, O Wisdom from on high
(Tenor) O come, O come thou Lord of Might
(Soprano) O come, O Shoot of Jesse free

(Bass) O come, O come, Emmanuel
(Quartet) Rejoice, Rejoice, Emmanuel
Shall come to thee, O Israel.
O come, O come, O come, O come, O come, O come,

(Soprano) O come, let us adore him,
(Soprano and Alto) O come, let us adore him,
(Quartet) O come, let us adore him, Christ the Lord!

Carol   "O Come, All Ye Faithful"

Postlude

Christmas Antiphon Organ Accompaniment

Arranged by Jeffey Whitman

Christmas Antiphon

Arranged by Jeffey Whitman

Lyrics underlaid in the music:

Line (mm. 10–14):
- S: joice, Re - joice, Em - man - u - el Shall come to thee, O Is - ra -
- A: joice, Re - joice, Em - man - u - el Shall come to thee, O Is - ra -
- T: joice, Re - joice, Em - man - u - el Shall come to thee, O Is - ra
- B: joice, Re - joice, Em - man - u - el Shall come to thee, O Is - ra -

Line (mm. 15–):
- S: el. O come, let us a -
- A: el. O come, O come,
- T: el. O come, O come,
- B: el. O come, O come,

Lyrics under the music:

Soprano (m. 20): dore him, O come, let us a - dore him, O come, let us a - dore him,

Alto (m. 20): O come, let us a - dore him, O come, let us a - dore him,

Tenor (m. 20): O come, let us a - dore him,

Bass (m. 20): O come, let us a - dore him,

Soprano (m. 25): Christ _____ the Lord!

Alto (m. 25): Christ _____ the Lord!

Tenor (m. 25): Christ _____ the Lord!

Bass (m. 25): Christ _____ the Lord!

Children's Sermons

Growing Up In God
and
Celebrating Jesus' Birth

Wesley T. Runk

Growing Up In God

Boys and girls, it is Christmas Eve. We are all here tonight to worship Jesus, the Christ and the Son of God. Isn't that special? *(let them answer)* If someone told you that the Christ was born somewhere near us, where would you go to look for him? *(let them answer)* Would you look in your guest room at home? You know the room I am talking about — the one that is kept very nice and no one sleeps in unless your grandparents come to visit or you have a special guest. Would this be a nice place for Jesus to be born in tonight? *(let them answer)*

Of course, you don't have many animals stay in your guest bedroom, do you? *(let them answer)* Maybe the garage would be a better place? We could just move out the cars and some of the garden tools and I am sure the holy family could fit and there would be extra places for the animals. How does your garage sound to you? *(let them answer)*

When people come to my house, we almost always end up in the kitchen. The adults drink coffee and may even eat some chips and dip. The children usually have some kind of fruit drink and some snacks. I think we could make a place for Jesus in our kitchen. We would just move the table and chairs into a corner and bring in a cot and some baby blankets and I think it would work. We would leave a lot of milk in the refrigerator and have lots of things we could fix in the microwave. Of course, I don't know how we would get all of the angels in to sing their heavenly songs. How does the kitchen sound to you? *(let them answer)*

Maybe we should look next door at the neighbor's house. They have a swimming pool and it has a fence around it so it would be a little more private. The only problem is that it is at the back of the house and the shepherds are kind of shy people. I don't know if they would know how to start looking in people's backyards. But it would be a nice place for Joseph to stretch out and relax and occasionally take a dip. What do you think? *(let them answer)*

Have you picked out a favorite place at your house where Jesus could be born? *(let them answer)* My children suggested the holy family stay in the television room with them. The children spend most of their time in this room. They think Joseph and Mary would enjoy the cartoons. They even gave their beanbag chair for Jesus to sleep in if he wanted. What do you think about the television room? *(let them answer)* Personally, I don't know if Mary, Joseph, and Jesus are into television.

Well, I think it is time to pick where you think Jesus would be born if he was born tonight in our town. Have you thought about where Jesus would be born in our town or in your neighborhood? *(let them answer)* By the way, you remember that each Wise Man brought Jesus a special gift. What kind of special gift would you give to Jesus if you were present the night when Jesus was born? *(let them answer)*

These are some of the things I think about when I read the Bible about the birth of Jesus. When you go home tonight, before you go to bed, ask your mom or dad to read you the story of the birth of Jesus from the Gospel of Luke. God bless you, and may all of your days be spent with the Christmas child. Amen.

Celebrating Jesus' Birth

Welcome, children. Today is the day we celebrate the birth of Jesus. We call it Christmas because we worship Jesus as God sent him to us. Do you remember where Jesus was born? *(let them answer)* He was born in an inn in the city of Bethlehem. Do you remember the place at the inn where Jesus was born? *(let them answer)* Very good, it was a stable that had a crib filled with hay.

Was anyone there when Jesus was born? *(let them answer)* There was Mary and Joseph, the parents of Jesus. Who else? *(let them answer)* Shepherds, there were several shepherds. Do you think maybe they brought one of the baby sheep from the fields? *(let them answer)* Who else was there? *(let them answer)* The donkey that brought Mary to the inn must have been given a place in the stable, don't you think? I think the donkey received some extra oats and hay to eat that night. And then there were the other barn animals like the cows, sheep, and maybe even some special animals like camels. Camels were a favorite way for people to ride from one town to another, and I know that there must have been some birds and maybe even a little mouse. Birds and mice are in almost every barn that I have ever seen.

Have we missed anyone? *(let them answer)* That's right, the angels, including Gabriel. The angels were heard singing and praising God out in the fields. The Bible calls them the heavenly host. Can you imagine the wonderful sound of angels singing? *(let them answer)* It would be great to hear a chorus of angels singing. I would go anywhere to hear that kind of concert. I didn't forget the star, did I? Or later on, the Wise Men from the East?

Isn't it amazing how Jesus draws us all together? Many members of families travel hundreds of miles to be together on this night. It is one of the most special nights of any year, as we wait to hear the announcement that Jesus Christ, son of Mary, is born into our world to bring us joy, forgiveness, and a brand-new kingdom.

The Bible spoke of this day hundreds of years before Jesus was ever born. They called this child, "Wonderful, Counselor, Prince of Peace." He was born of the Holy Spirit and people dreamed of him coming.

This is a very holy day. Jesus is the greatest gift ever given by God. Today we worship him as a tiny baby — with shepherds, camels, donkeys, cows, sheep, angels, and a star. The Bible doesn't mention the birds or the mice, but if they were there they also worshiped Jesus.

When you open your presents, perhaps you will say a prayer to God, thanking him for sending Jesus, the greatest of all gifts and the one that brings angels, people, and all of the animals in the world together.

Merry Christmas, God's children, Merry Christmas to all. Amen.

www.ingramcontent.com/pod-product-compliance
Lightning Source LLC
LaVergne TN
LVHW061341060426

835511LV00014B/2043